YEAR__________ MONTHS

CLASS MEMBERS' NAMES DATES

Number of teachers present

Number of class members present

Number of visitors present

Total present

Offering

Using This Book

Record books are a useful tool for Sunday school and other classes. With enough room for an entire year's worth of information, class leaders can evaluate attendance and locate member contact information quickly and easily.

Stay Connected!

Set a regular time to review your record book. Take note of class members and their level of participation. As you guide your class in their Christian growth, you will find it beneficial to build relationships and to support and encourage each other.

- Make a point of periodically contacting your class members. Follow up on prayer requests, share future class plans, and ask for feedback. You may choose to pay a visit, make a short phone call, mail a card or note, or send a text or e-mail. This personal contact lets people know they are important to you and to the class.
- Contact members who have been absent for a while. Just knowing that they were missed will often be the encouragement that brings someone back to class.
- Reach out to first-time guests and let them know you appreciated their visit to your class. Invite them to come again and allow them to share any needs or concerns they may have.
- Be consistent and keep your class connections strong. People make an effort to attend when they feel welcome and wanted, and they often invite their friends to come as well.

Connection Summary for the Year

Record total number of contacts/visits made each week.

MONTH						
1.						
2.						
3.						
4.						
5.						
	QUARTERLY TOTAL			**QUARTERLY TOTAL**		

MONTH						
1.						
2.						
3.						
4.						
5.						
	QUARTERLY TOTAL			**QUARTERLY TOTAL**		

YEAR__________	MONTHS				
CLASS MEMBERS' NAMES	DATES				

LISTING OF CLASS MEMBERS

NAMES	ADDRESSES	PHONES
	Home: e-mail:	Home: Cell Phone:
	Home: e-mail:	Home: Cell Phone:
	Home: e-mail:	Home: Cell Phone:
	Home: e-mail:	Home: Cell Phone:
	Home: e-mail:	Home: Cell Phone:
	Home: e-mail:	Home: Cell Phone:
	Home: e-mail:	Home: Cell Phone:
	Home: e-mail:	Home: Cell Phone:
	Home: e-mail:	Home: Cell Phone:
	Home: e-mail:	Home: Cell Phone:
	Home: e-mail:	Home: Cell Phone:
	Home: e-mail:	Home: Cell Phone:
	Home: e-mail:	Home: Cell Phone:
	Home: e-mail:	Home: Cell Phone:
	Home: e-mail:	Home: Cell Phone:
	Home: e-mail:	Home: Cell Phone:
	Home: e-mail:	Home: Cell Phone:
	Home: e-mail:	Home: Cell Phone:
	Home: e-mail:	Home: Cell Phone:
	Home: e-mail:	Home: Cell Phone:
	Home: e-mail:	Home: Cell Phone:
	Home: e-mail:	Home: Cell Phone:
	Home: e-mail:	Home: Cell Phone:
	Home: e-mail:	Home: Cell Phone:
	Home: e-mail:	Home: Cell Phone:
	Home: e-mail:	Home: Cell Phone:

LISTING OF CLASS MEMBERS

NAMES	ADDRESSES	PHONES
	Home: e-mail:	Home: Cell Phone:
	Home: e-mail:	Home: Cell Phone:
	Home: e-mail:	Home: Cell Phone:
	Home: e-mail:	Home: Cell Phone:
	Home: e-mail:	Home: Cell Phone:
	Home: e-mail:	Home: Cell Phone:
	Home: e-mail:	Home: Cell Phone:
	Home: e-mail:	Home: Cell Phone:
	Home: e-mail:	Home: Cell Phone:
	Home: e-mail:	Home: Cell Phone:
	Home: e-mail:	Home: Cell Phone:
	Home: e-mail:	Home: Cell Phone:
	Home: e-mail:	Home: Cell Phone:
	Home: e-mail:	Home: Cell Phone:
	Home: e-mail:	Home: Cell Phone:
	Home: e-mail:	Home: Cell Phone:
	Home: e-mail:	Home: Cell Phone:
	Home: e-mail:	Home: Cell Phone:
	Home: e-mail:	Home: Cell Phone:
	Home: e-mail:	Home: Cell Phone:
	Home: e-mail:	Home: Cell Phone:
	Home: e-mail:	Home: Cell Phone:
	Home: e-mail:	Home: Cell Phone:
	Home: e-mail:	Home: Cell Phone:
	Home: e-mail:	Home: Cell Phone:
	Home: e-mail:	Home: Cell Phone:

ATTENDANCE SUMMARY FOR THE YEAR

	FALL QUARTER			WINTER QUARTER			SPRING QUARTER			SUMMER QUARTER		
	Members	Visitors	Total	Members	Visitors	Total	Members	Visitors	Total	Members	Visitors	Total
1.												
2.												
3.												
4.												
5.												
6.												
7.												
8.												
9.												
10.												
11.												
12.												
13.												
Total												

ATTENDANCE TOTAL FOR THE YEAR MEMBERS_______________ VISITORS_______________ GRAND TOTAL_______________